LET'S MAKE

Carol Jones
illustrated by Craig Smith

"So.... how about it? Let's make a deal."

ASHTON SCHOLASTIC
SYDNEY AUCKLAND NEW YORK TORONTO LONDON

Jones, Carol, 1957–.

Let's Make a Deal.

    ISBN 1 86388 354 1.

    1. Money—History—Juvenile literature. I. Smith, Craig, 1955–.
II. Title. (Series: Mathshelf.)

332.4

Text copyright © Carol Jones, 1995.

Illustrations copyright © Ashton Scholastic Pty Limited, 1995.

First published in 1995 by Ashton Scholastic Pty Limited
A.C.N. 000 614 577, PO Box 579, Gosford 2250. Also in Brisbane,
Melbourne, Adelaide, Perth and Auckland, NZ.

All rights reserved. No part of this publication may be reproduced or
transmitted in any form or by any means, electronic or mechanical,
including photocopying, recording, storage in an information retrieval
system, or otherwise, without the prior written permission of the
publisher, unless specifically permitted under the Australian
Copyright Act 1968 as amended.

Typeset in Vag Rounded Thin.

Printed in Singapore through Global Com Pte Ltd.

9 8 7 6 5 4 3 2 1   5 6 7 8 / 9

CONTENTS

Swaps	4
To barter, to barter	7
Funny money	11
Metal money	17
Coins and notes	20
Make me an offer	25
Money in the bank	28
Plastic money	31
The Future	32

SWAPS

You can't pay for the toy of your dreams with your old Lego. (Lego doesn't fit in the cash register for one thing!) But your friend next door might swap one of her Matchbox cars for one of your favourite books.

Mostly, you use money when you buy things at shops because the shopkeepers don't want your goods. When you have something your friends want and they have something you want, you can swap. A fair deal or exchange is one where you both agree that the goods are of equal value.

MONEY BOX

You've probably swapped lunches with friends many times. What else might you swap? What do you do if you think your goods are more valuable than theirs?

Sometimes you might exchange one service for another. If you want your mother to take you to the hottest new movie in town she might ask you to do something for her in return. When you swap, you need to have a discussion to find a deal which suits both of you.

MONEY BOX

Your mum will take you to the movies if you do something for her in return.

She gives you three choices. You can

- a) *wash the kitchen and bathroom floors*
- b) *weed the front garden*
- c) *clean the car, inside and out.*

How will you decide? Should you choose the easiest for you? The quickest? The most fun? Do you think your choice would be the same as everyone else's? Survey your friends to find out.

TO BARTER, TO BARTER

Stone-age people didn't carry wallets. They didn't have money to put in them. When one person needed something another person had, they traded or bartered for it: dried fish for mammoth steaks; bone needles for wooden bowls; animal furs for flint axe heads.

For thousands of years people bartered for goods. Merchants travelled vast distances by camel, horse or ship to barter with merchants in other lands.

The ancient Egyptians didn't have very much timber, but they had plenty of linen woven from the flax growing by the Nile. They bartered their linen for timber from Lebanon. The people of ancient Crete made beautiful bronze weapons, but they needed metals to make them. They bartered their weapons for the metals and grains of Cyprus, Sicily and Spain.

MONEY BOX

You are an Egyptian merchant with 10 metres of fine linen. You say your linen is worth three times as much as a metre of sturdy timber from Lebanon. A Lebanese merchant says linen and timber are equal in value. How much timber do you want for the 10 metres of linen? How much timber does the Lebanese merchant wish to barter? How could you make a deal? Perhaps you could even act out their conversation with a partner.

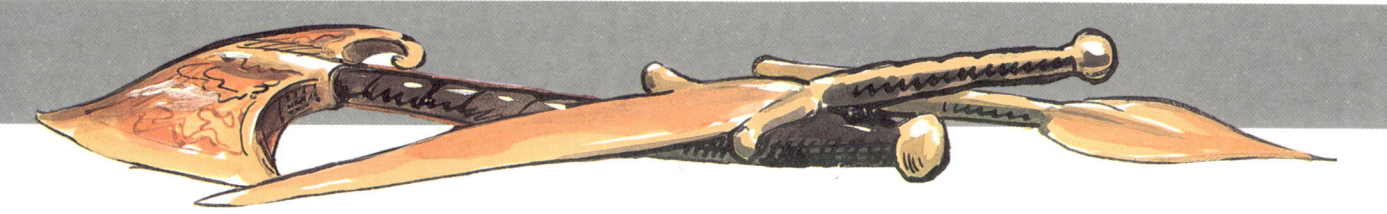

Throughout history, people bartered what they had plenty of for what they needed. The Diyari people of Lake Eyre in South Australia, for example, walked hundreds of kilometres to swap boomerangs, spears and nets for a special red earth to decorate their bodies and tools. Shells from the Gulf of Carpentaria in the north were swapped many times on their way to the Diyari, halfway across the continent of Australia.

In some places, people even bartered for their rent. Peasants might trade work on the lord of the manor's fields for the rent they owed him. Or they might pay in grain they had grown.

Barter can be very useful. But before you ask for your pocket money in chocolate bars, think about this. What if the other person doesn't want what you have? A tailor might not want the fish a fisherman has to offer. Even if the tailor does want the fish, how do they measure the value of a fish against a coat? And what happens if they decide a fish is worth only one quarter of a coat? A single sleeve isn't much use to anyone. Barter isn't always as easy as it seems.

MONEY BOX

If you were the fisherman and agreed with the tailor that a fish is worth only one quarter of a coat, how could you make a deal so that you got your coat?

FUNNY MONEY

Would you buy a barrel of pickled nightingales' tongues or a truckload of seaweed biscuits? Yuck! That's the trouble when you have what only a very few people want. It's hard to find customers. So how do you barter with all the other people who have things you want?

People around the world solved this problem by using something that everyone in their part of the world thought valuable. In many places this was cows and oxen—cattle. Cows provided milk and meat. Oxen could pull ploughs and carts. They were valuable to all. A merchant with pickled nightingale tongues could barter for cows when the queen bought a couple of barrels of tongues for a big party at the palace. Later, he could trade one of his cows for a new cart. The cows were like funny four-legged money.

Cattle weren't the only funny money. Soon after the British settled in Australia they found they didn't have enough coins to go around. It was a very long trip back to England to get more coins, so for money they used something all the convicts and soldiers wanted—rum! In 1790, the road from Sydney to Liverpool cost 400 gallons (1800 litres) of rum to build.

FUNNY MONEY IN HISTORY

Barley	Sumer
Butter	Norway
Cattle	Rome, Greece, Kenya, India, Iran
Cigarettes	Prisoner-of-war camps during World War II
Elephants	Sri Lanka
Fish hooks	Gilbert Islands
Furs	Alaska, Canada, Mongolia, Russia, Scandinavia
Human skulls	Borneo
Knives	China
Pigs	Indonesia
Rats	Easter Island
Rice	India
Rum	Australia
Salt	Nigeria, Ethiopia, ancient Rome
Shells	Solomon Islands, Thailand, China, Africa
Stones	Yap Islands
Tobacco	Virginia
Whale teeth	Fiji

MONEY BOX

At a market in old Norway you want to buy two dozen eggs, a sack of potatoes, a pair of shoes and two apples. How much butter will you need to barter?

EGGS = 1 kilo butter per dozen

SACK OF POTATOES = 3 kilos of butter

CHEAP

SHOES = 8 kilos of butter a pair

APPLES = 8 for a kilo of butter

Of course, not all types of funny money worked as well as others. Cattle aren't all of equal value and they can be divided only if they're dead. Human skulls are in short supply. Elephants are difficult to carry. Butter can melt. Fish hooks can be dangerous in pockets.

MONEY BOX

Work out your own funny money system with a friend. Remember, it needs to be something that people in your class think is valuable or useful—pencils, basketball cards, stickers. What would you use? Once you've decided, work out an exchange system. How much funny money would some common items in your classroom be worth?

Money needs to be acceptable. Fish hooks won't pay the bills if you're living in a desert. Who needs them? And shells are not valuable if the local beach is littered with them. Funny money might be accepted by local people but not by people far away.

Money needs to be acceptable, and people need to be able to measure it so they know how much it's worth. That means they must be able to count or weigh it.

Money also needs to be easy to handle. Some types of funny money, such as the huge stone discs of the Yap Islands, would be too big and heavy to transport easily.

It must be possible to divide money into smaller units. And money often needs to be stored for later use, so funny money such as butter is not ideal because it doesn't last.

METAL MONEY

One kind of money which is acceptable, measurable, easy to handle, divisible and storable is metal money—like the coins we use today.

People have been using metal money in some parts of the world for 4000 years. But, unlike a coin, you couldn't put this metal money in your piggy bank. It came in all shapes and sizes and was not shaped like a coin at all. There were rings and rods, lumps and wires, bars and ingots, hoes, even animal shapes.

Don't spend it all at once.

For this kind of money shopkeepers needed scales like a greengrocer uses, because the metal was weighed, not counted. Sometimes this was because the metal could come in any shape or size. Even though the bars or ingots started out in regular sizes, dishonest people sometimes chipped off little bits. If they chipped away at enough ingots they could make a few of their own!

METAL MONEY IN HISTORY

Animal shapes	Egypt, Assyria
Copper rings	Nigeria
Copper lumps	Rome
Gold and silver rings	Egypt, Ireland
Gold dust	Ghana, and USA, Canada and Australia during gold rushes
Iron hoes	Sudan, China
Iron rods	Liberia
Silver ingots	China, Syria, Japan
Silver wire	Sri Lanka

MONEY BOX

You want to sell your prize camel. One buyer wants to pay in gold rings. One wants to pay in silver ingots. The third will pay in copper bars. In today's money, imagine that the gold is worth $13 a gram, the silver is worth $3 a gram and the copper is worth 2 cents a gram. How much is each buyer offering in today's money?

Which offer should you accept?

a) 10 grams of gold
b) 37 grams of silver
c) 7 kilograms of copper?
(1 kilogram = 1000 grams)

COINS AND NOTES

More than 2600 years ago in Turkey, traders in the city of Lydia had a golden idea. Instead of weighing metal money, they decided to mark small pieces of metal with a money value. Then they stamped the pieces with an impression of a lion's head. The stamp promised or guaranteed the Lydians would buy the pieces back for that value. They had invented coins!

MONEY BOX

Look at a collection of different coins. What is on all of them? Is there something common to each? What different pictures are there on each of the coins?

Not long after this, coins were also invented in China. And the Lydians' good idea spread around the Mediterranean Sea and even to India. Rulers of cities or states could then make coins marked with their own special designs guaranteeing the value.

Most early coins were what we call 'standard' coins. The value stamped on the coin was equal to the value of the metal. In England, King Henry III made sure his coins were the same weight or 'standard' by measuring them against grains of wheat. Each silver penny had to weigh the same as 24 grains of wheat.

Today we use 'token' coins. The metal in our coins is worth less than the value stamped on the coin. But people accept the coins because they are guaranteed by the government.

MONEY BOX

Some countries use dollars and cents. Each dollar is divided into 100 cents. France has francs and centimes. Japan uses yen. Each country has its own 'currency' or money. Find out what people in other countries call their money. Is it divided into hundreds like our dollar? Do they put the same picture on one side of all their coins? Parents might have coins from other countries at home and banks often have information about other currencies. The encyclopedias in your library will also help. Find out as much as you can.

It can ta... ...e to count the money in your piggy bank, especially if it's full. And it could be pretty heavy to carry all those coins around. Imagine what would happen if your parents had to pay their bills and do all the shopping with coins.

Paper money or bank notes make it easier to move money around and they are useful when metals are scarce. The first bank notes were made more than 900 years ago in China because there was a shortage of copper and the less valuable iron coins were too heavy.

Paper money is convenient, but the paper itself is worthless. Paper money is accepted only if it is guaranteed by a government or a respected bank. Monopoly money won't pay for the groceries!

MAKE ME AN OFFER

One way in which shops attract buyers is by holding sales. They reduce the prices of goods in the store. Sometimes the price tag is marked down by a certain number of dollars or cents. Sometimes the store advertises goods at half the usual price. And sometimes the store offers a ten per cent, twenty-five per cent, even a fifty per cent discount or reduction. If a store advertises a ten per cent discount the goods will be 10/100 (or one tenth) cheaper. A twenty-five per cent discount means the goods will be 25/100 (or one quarter) cheaper, and a fifty per cent discount means the goods will be 50/100 (or one half) cheaper.

MONEY BOX

Three shops have a sale on shirts. The shirts were all $30 each. Now the Generous Jeans store is giving a 10 per cent discount. Al's Menswear has marked its shirts down 30 per cent and the Shirt Factory is giving a 20 per cent discount. Which shop has the cheapest shirts? How much money would you save if you bought three shirts from this store?

Supermarkets always have 'specials'. These 'specials' are cheaper than the usual price for these items. The supermarkets hope customers will come to buy the specials and stay to buy all their groceries.

MONEY BOX

Visit the supermarket or read a supermarket ad in the newspaper. Find ten items on special. What are the usual prices for these items? What are the special prices? How much money would you save if you bought one of each item?

Buyers can ask sellers for a discount, or offer less than the asking price. Sellers may agree, disagree or suggest another price altogether. Buyers can accept this or try again with another offer. Trying to agree on a special price like this is called bargaining.

In many parts of the world, people often bargain when they buy expensive items such as houses or cars. In some countries, people bargain over everything! Shopping could take longer but would certainly be more fun.

MONEY IN THE BANK

Some people store their money at home, but then they find it is too easy to spend, or that it may even be stolen. Most people keep their money in banks so that they can deposit it, keep it safe and save it until they need to withdraw it.

MONEY BOX

If you have a bank account, look back at your passbook or bank statements. How much money have you deposited in the last year? This will be in the credit column. How much have you withdrawn? This will be in the debit column.

Another reason why people keep their money in banks is that banks pay to look after it. This payment is called interest. Interest is paid as a percentage of the money in your bank account. Five per cent interest each year means the bank pays you five cents for every 100 cents (one dollar) in your account.

MONEY BOX

If five per cent interest on one dollar is five cents, how much is five per cent interest on ten dollars? How much is five per cent interest on one hundred dollars?

Banks not only look after your money, they also lend it out to other people. When banks lend people money (the money they are looking after for customers), they expect to get it back—with interest!

The longer borrowers keep money, the more interest they pay the bank. And the higher the interest rate, the more money they have to pay back. Some people end up repaying two or three times the amount they borrowed!

MONEY BOX

Banks offer different rates of interest. Check through some newspaper advertisements to find which bank and type of account has the highest interest rate. Which has the lowest? If you kept $100 in each account for a whole year, how much interest would you earn at the highest rate and at the lowest rate?

PLASTIC MONEY

People found that paper money was lighter and easier to carry than funny money like cattle, or even coins. These days money seems so light, people can carry all the money they own on a single plastic card!

The cards aren't really money. That's being looked after by the bank. But the card and busy computers let them withdraw money from their bank accounts without actually touching notes or coins. The computers record money moving from the buyer's account to the seller's account. This is called a debit card.

People can also make payments with cheques. A cheque is like an order to your bank to pay money from your account to another person.

Another kind of card is called a credit card. Instead of taking money from your bank account, a credit card lets you borrow money from the bank. Of course the bank wants the money back—with interest!

Little plastic cards are more convenient than bars of iron or blocks of butter. They make it easy to measure, divide and pay money, and they are simple to store. But like any form of money they will work only if they are accepted.

THE FUTURE

Who knows what money will look like tomorrow? Perhaps plastic cards will be replaced by minicomputers which will allow us to transfer the money from our bank account directly to the shop from which we are purchasing the goods. Anyway, money, cards or computers, it's still fun to make a deal!